CODPIECES

Perry Pontac

CODPIECES

a triple bill

With a foreword
by Alan Bennett

OBERON BOOKS
LONDON

WWW.OBERONBOOKS.COM

First published in this collection in 2011 by Oberon Books Ltd
521 Caledonian Road, London N7 9RH
Tel: +44 (0) 20 7607 3637 / Fax: +44 (0) 20 7607 3629
e-mail: info@oberonbooks.com
www.oberonbooks.com

A catalogue record for this book is available from the British
Library.

ISBN: 978-1-84943-055-5

Cover illustration by James Illman.

Printed in Great Britain by CPI Antony Rowe, Chippenham.

For Sanelra

Contents

Foreword

The plays of Perry Pontac have been a well-kept secret on BBC radio for far too long. They have been turning up regularly on what I'm afraid I still call the wireless ever since 1987 but it's only with *Codpieces*, comprising three of Pontac's Shakespearean parodies, that they now at last find their way into print.

Parodies they are but told in the form of prefaces and continuations… what happens after Fortinbras turns up at the end of *Hamlet* or before Lear takes it into his head to share out his kingdom; say Romeo and Juliet didn't die, what is in store for them 20 years down the road? Pontac stands to the side of these familiar masterpieces, treating them with irony rather than disrespect and in language so close to Shakespeare's that it's a while before the penny drops and one realises this is parody of the highest order.

Now I am no stranger to Shakespearean parody, a sample of which was one of the highlights of *Beyond The Fringe*, the revue with which my career started back in 1960. And it was very funny, but reading Perry Pontac's Shakespeare I am (only slightly) mortified to find that he can write cod Shakespeare much better than Peter Cook, Jonathan Miller, Dudley Moore or myself.

No one, though, can parody anything… an author, a composer, a singer, a style… without initial love and delight. Parody comes out of affection; it is an homage and the nearer a parody adjoins its object the better it is. Perry Pontac would be Shakespeare if he could so instead he simulates him so exactly that it's only gradually one realises how gloriously silly it is.

And it isn't easy. Peter Cook used to think he could extemporise Shakespeare but it was always dire and indeed an embarrassment whereas with Pontac one has to keep remembering this isn't the Bard, so close is the language to the real article.

Of the late Laertes, for instance:

> 'A corpse who even now
> Is freshly festering in a nearby grave
> With all the zest of youth.'

Or in *Fatal Loins*:

(The Nurse speaks of caring for Juliet's numberless children):

> 'I needs must groom their thickly knotted hair;
> They scream at first, then smile to look so fair.
> For combing is a kind of pleasant woe,
> And parting such sweet sorrow. I must go'

Another prerequisite of successful parody is that the writer should know more than his or her audience... but only a little more. There would be no sense, for instance, in sending up Shakespearean sonnet forms to an audience unversed in them. Whereas an audience knows what Shakespeare sounds like without (and I speak from the heart) always understanding what is being said. And in that gap lies parody.

Pontac's fantasy is as exuberant as his language, with gender a mere trifle. The grizzled Kent reveals to Lear that he is and has always been, a woman, whereupon Lear falls for him on the spot:

> 'Kent: My voice was ever low
> An excellent thing in woman, as you know.
> And years of drinking sack and heavy mead
> Have delved for me a deeper voice indeed.'

'All the fault of that damned padre' was Nancy Mitford's Uncle Matthew's response when he was taken to *Romeo and Juliet*. He might well have preferred the Pontac version in which Romeo survives the tomb only to cherish a lifelong passion for the bumbling friar:

> 'Romeo: Thy tonsure – that sweet circle past compare,
> Like a pink lotus in a sea of hair.
> Thy noble ankles and the very toes
> That peep out of thy sandals in neat rows'

Sublimely silly though they may be Pontac's plays do have

what are now quite venerable ancestors with some of his wilder imaginings not unrelated to the kind of sketches that always used to be on in the West End when I was young… *Sweet and Low, Airs on a Shoestring, Pieces of Eight…* the kind of revues which, alas, *Beyond the Fringe* killed off. They have radio antecedents too as there are echoes here of the idiosyncratic comedy of Peter Ustinov and Peter Jones, *In All Directions*, in the early days of the Third Programme. Henry Reed is another forebear, the sagas of Hilda Tablet in the same strain of intellectual comedy. Though of course one must not say so… intellectual is not a word the BBC would welcome attached to comedy (or anything else much).

If I have a criticism (and I don't) it would be that Pontac occasionally permits himself a dreadful joke. But then so do I so I'll keep quiet.

The plays printed here are only three of Perry Pontac's large and varied output. I hope these will just be the first of many that will now find their way into print and that this may lead to their performance on the stage. So skilful and silly they are a gift to actors and a tonic for audiences. Nobody else is doing this. They should be seen.

Alan Bennett, 2011

HAMLET, PART II

a sequel to Shakespeare's *Hamlet, Part I*

Hamlet, Part II (1992) was broadcast on BBC Radio Three. The cast was as follows:

FORNIA, Harriet Walter
SELTAZAR, Peter Jeffrey
THE FOOL, Simon Russell Beale
THE KING, John Moffatt

Directed by Richard Wortley

Characters

FORNIA

SELTAZAR

A FOOL

THE KING

HAMLET, PART II

(Elsinore. A platform before the castle. From one side of the stage SELTAZAR *enters, and from the other* FORNIA, *who, on seeing* SELTAZAR, *rushes to offer him her hand in hearty greeting.)*

FORNIA: Welcome, good Seltazar, at last returned
From foreign realms, thy mission done and blest
With fortune's fruitage and the palms of peace.
All Elsinore this greeting gives to thee
With one unstinting universal tongue.

SELTAZAR: I thank thee, Fornia. Welcome do I feel
After my three years absence. I have been
Ambassador too long in lands remote
In loyal service to the Danish crown;
And here before the castle's ramparts high
My heart doth leap, like to the roistering vole
In native glades delighting. For I yearn
To taste again the joys of this, my home,
The sound of jovial cannons and of song,
Of merriment and wassail; and the sight
Of royal splendour, tournament and feast.
I have been starved of pleasures – and of news.
(Eagerly.) Tell me, I pray, how goes the Danish state?
What toys, what changes, fashions, shifts and turns?
(With deep affection.) And how is Hamlet, Denmark's
    dear delight?
Young Hamlet, witty, jocund, kind and free,
Of liberal heart and manner nobly sweet,
Poetic Hamlet, hope of all the land,
Life of our life and loadstar of our fate,
Dancer, mimic, soldier, raconteur,

Philosopher and favourite of the gods.

FORNIA: *(With difficulty.)* Hamlet, my lord … is dead.
(Pause.)

SELTAZAR: *(Shocked.)* What? Hamlet dead?
Alas! but how came Hamlet thus to die?

FORNIA: Young Hamlet died in duelling, gentle sir.
He fought the young Laertes, also dead.

SELTAZAR: *(Appalled.)* Laertes dead?

FORNIA: A corpse who even now
Is freshly festering in a nearby grave
With all the zest of youth.

SELTAZAR: How did he die?

FORNIA: In combat keen against our former Prince
For vengeance of his sister, lately mad.

SELTAZAR: The fair Ophelia?

FORNIA: *Foul* Ophelia, sir.
For she lies decomposing, though her wits
Rotted before her. 'Twas her father's death.

SELTAZAR: The fair Polonius?

FORNIA: Dead, sir, dead as well.
Slain by Prince Hamlet who, as you have heard,
Is also dead.

SELTAZAR: How tragic for the Queen.

FORNIA: Gertrude, I fear, has passed beyond such pain,
Plucked off by poison from the King's own hand.

SELTAZAR: Is't possible? King Claudius, he who reigns?

FORNIA: Who *reigned*, my friend, for he is quite reigned out.
Young Hamlet too hath heaved him up to Heaven.

SELTAZAR: And Hamlet's father?

FORNIA: Deader than the rest:
He died before the killing had begun.
He's now a ghost, and often can be heard
Intoning on these very battlements.

SELTAZAR: *(Desperately)* And Osric, the effeminate courtier?

FORNIA: Dead of exertion following the duel.
(SELTAZAR groans in general grief.)

FORNIA: A hideous scene of blood and, as I fear,
A heavy sight to greet young Fortinbras.

SELTAZAR: Young Fortinbras?

FORNIA: The conquering prince who came,
Moonlike, to view the slaughter of the field,
Pale monarch of the slumbering citadel –
Inheritor of Denmark's empty crown.
(Pause.)

SELTAZAR: So Fortinbras is king in Denmark now.
How is he?

FORNIA: He is dead, my lord, as well.

SELTAZAR: How came he too to die? It seems most strange.

FORNIA: Struck dead by all the news of all the dead.
The fatal tidings shocked his delicate spirit
And called it to repose. He died soon after
He heard the bloody summary from the lips
Of Horatio. The late Horatio.

SELTAZAR: Alas Horatio! And is he gone as well?
Horatio, the Prince's consort and his pride?
His linkèd shadow and his fortune's stave,

His loyal aid and comfort and defence?

FORNIA: Gone, gone, my lord, to dally in the dust.
No sooner had he voiced his bitter tale
Than, taking out the sword he ever kept
For just such moments, plunged it with a sigh
Into the scabbard of his heaving heart
And, shortly, slept.

SELTAZAR: *(Greatly moved.)* O grievous anecdote!

FORNIA: And others too have ta'en their loyal lives
With swords and bodkins, cannons, spears and knives:
Marcellus and Bernardo and a Priest,
Reynaldo and Francisco and the Players,
A gentleman, a Captain and two Clowns –
The 'Dramatis Personae', as it were.

SELTAZAR: But of the Royal Family …?

FORNIA: They all
Have perished, fled into the passing clouds.
The floor a field of ruffles and of blood,
Of tights and doublets of a hundred hues,
Of royal crowns and sceptres by the score.

SELTAZAR: When did this happen?

FORNIA: But last Saturday.

SELTAZAR: O horrible! Most horrible, Fornia!
But where, I pray, are now these kingly corpses?
These fallen meteors of expiréd light?
I toured the castle, cellarage to rampart,
And didst behold no such unearthly sight,
So hellish that mine eyes would shrink to see
And, like the rebel angels in their plight,

        Dive deep within the furrows of my face.

FORNIA: It hardly would be seemly, O my lord,
        To leave them there midst blood and gore and sword
        And bowel and bone, a princely abattoir.
        No, all are resting in the chapel now,
        The Royal Tombs at full capacity.

SELTAZAR: *(Sighing.)* So, none survives.

FORNIA: None, Seltazar.

SELTAZAR: Alas. *(He grieves briefly.)*
        But who will fill the throne now all are gone?
        Old Hamlet, and Young Hamlet, and the Queen,
        Young Fortinbras and Claudius – none remains
        To wear the crown of Denmark and to guide
        Its fretful destiny. O Gods! What trials
        You set us mortals in our own despite.
        For what succession now could e'er succeed?
        What loyalty to royalty can spring?
        What blossom can attend the blighted flower
        When no bud beckons to the summer's sun?
        (Pointedly.) Where no crown crowns, no knee can need to
            kneel.
        Denmark will fall to anarchy at last.
        Or common curs with sweaty neckerchiefs,
        Swine-filthy rogues with dirty fingernails,
        Bad breath and local accents and poor teeth
        Will climb into the golden chairs of state,
        Cramming rich crowns upon their greasy locks,
        And give command to base rebellion.
        O! that some prince of wise experience
        Held title to adopt this orphaned land.

FORNIA: I have, my lord, bethought me on this theme,
And, as the head librarian of the Court,
For several days I have immersed myself
Deep in the royal records of the realm.

SELTAZAR: Hast thou, my Fornia?

FORNIA: Yes indeed, my lord. *(Pause.)*
(Excitedly.) O Seltazar, there is a man of hope,
A foreign monarch who doth bear a claim –
Slight as a cobweb, brittle as a bone,
Faint as a footfall, cumulus as a cloud,
Yet undeniable – a claim to rule
In Denmark, and a head to wear its crown.
(She unrolls a scroll.)
See on this scroll in antique letters writ:
His ancestor Lucestes was the sire
Of swart Antonica, a maiden aunt
Of hardy Scanafron, the sometime Prince
Of Caledonia West and brother-in-law
Of Sicolus, the mother of Verbena,
Half-sister to Fabèscarand the Bold,
Step-cousin to old Hamlet's father's niece.

SELTAZAR: *(Joyously.)* But this is news that plucks a wild huzzah
From any loyal heart that beats in Denmark.
Who is this man?

FORNIA: A native, sir, of Scotia.
A monarch lavish in his country's love,
Wise, fair and honest, brave and true and kind,
A soldier and a statesman of renown:
Noble Macbeth.

SELTAZAR: *(Shaken.)* Alas! You say, 'Macbeth'?
I late have been in Scotland, and I fear
Macbeth is dead.

FORNIA: *(Her hopes blasted.)* Macbeth dead? Can it be?

SELTAZAR: Past doubting. *(With interest.)* 'Twas a very curious death:
Slain by a forest, so the people say,
From Birnam come to far-off Dusinane.

FORNIA: *(Scornfully.)* Slain by a *florist*? A wretched death indeed.
I grieve for Scotland in her hour of shame.

SELTAZAR: Not 'florist' – nay but 'forest'; though indeed
'Florist' doth seem the likelier of the two.

FORNIA: *(Suddenly hopeful again.)* And of his wife? He had a wife, I
trow:
Lady Macbeth.

SELTAZAR: Ay, 'Jocelyn' by name.
She first went mad, then died, so no luck there.
(Forestalling further inquiries.) And Duncan too, and
Banquo. Ask no more.

FORNIA: So all is lost and past the bounds of hope.
But lo! Look, on the fringe of that fair hill
Dappled with daisies and wild columbine,
With nettle rank and fulsome gillyflowers,
With mottlewort and lusty maiden smock,
With violets damp and pumpkins all aglow,
Comes, running with fleetness like the meadow hare
When followed by the fierce and feral fox,
A man attired in motley, tattered weeds,
And nodding cap of bells upon his head.
Perhaps he brings us news of some lost heir,
Some long-forgotten prince to grace our throne,
Stolen by pirates in his infancy,
Then shipwrecked on a foreign strand, and raised
By marmosets in Patagonia.
(Clinging to this slender hope.) O happy chance if only it be
so!

(Enter a Fool, in traditional motley and jingling bells.)

SELTAZAR: *(Darkly.)* I fear he means some danger to the state.
Who are you, man – a rude rebellious hind
Here to plant treacherous plots, and thus confound
All exercise of custom and degree?
Beware lest thy reply I meet with steel.

THE FOOL: *(Country accent.)* I be a fool, sir, wandering here about,
Earning my humble living as I may
With witty jests and soul-bestirring songs.

SELTAZAR: *(Heartily grateful.)* A fool? O welcome, sir, to Elsinore!
Pray make us laugh with jolly japes and droll,
With sparkling puns and jests that charm the soul,
Shaking our frames with the earthquake merriment;
For we are deep in dark misfortune's shades,
Sad beyond sorrow, groaning beyond grief,
And seek the priceless palliative of laughter:
Abundant giggles, chortles of delight,
Amazéd joy to chase our sadness hence.

THE FOOL: I understand. I thus begin, my lord.
(He clears his throat extensively.) Why is a spring-cock
like a log-jam, nuncle? Because the longer the eaves-
beam the shorter the woof. 'Tis but hastening the owl's
commerce to deny it, my lord, though the rogue will
turn, yea spin till the globe itself grow giddy. And
yet men go a-dallying every day, though darkness
meet them in the guise of a peacock – or an hornéd
moon. And if a man have horns, by your leave, he be
behornéd. Watch to thy wife, my lord; she'll look after
thy horns.
(Pause.)

FORNIA: *(Softly, to SELTAZAR.)* Methinks I understood no single word.

SELTAZAR: *(Not perceptively amused.)* 'Tis very dry, his humour.

THE FOOL: 'Horns', you see.

People usually laugh at 'horns', my lord.
'Adultery', you know – a goodly jest.
When all else fails, I burp or mention 'horns'.
Or 'cuckoldry' or 'cuckoo!', something similar.
>   *(No reaction from the others.)*
(A trifle desperately.) I have a more extensive repertoire.
I slip and fall. I lose my pantaloons.
I walk into a tree and strike my head,
Then run about and shout in grievous pain,
Weeping full sore and bleeding copiously.
>   *(Still no reaction.)*
I make rude noises with my underarm.
I do an imitation of a duck …
Or chicken, sir – whichever takes your fancy:
A battery of never-failing tricks,
Reducing any company to mirth.

SELTAZAR: *(Judiciously)* I think perhaps not. Fornia …?

FORNIA: Thank you, no.
>   *(Pause.)*

THE FOOL: *(Hopefully.)* I sing a bit as well.

SELTAZAR: *(His interest reawakened.)* A song! A song!
Sing us a song, O fool, to make us wise,
Such as the fisher-folk in winter time
Sing as they sit and mend their humble nets
With frosty fingers aching, while their fire
Crackles beside them, and the scarlet loon
Sleeps in the branches of the banyan tree.

THE FOOL: I have *just* such a song, my lord, for you.
>   *(He clears his throat again and sings, rather tunelessly.)*
'Twas a willow and a swan,
Hey nonny no!
Youth will yield to age anon,
It must be so.

Flowers are fading like the moon,
Down derry down!
Simple maid and swain see soon
The leaves so brown.
Drop a tear or knoll a knell,
Tu-whit, tu-woo!
Lullaby and ding-dong-bell!
And cuckoo! too.
Fountains flow and birds take wing,
Heigh-ho and fie!
Jug-jug-jug! 'tis very spring,
And thus goodbye.
               (A pause.)

SELTAZAR: *(Unimpressed.)* Thank you then, fool. Here is a groat:
               now go.

THE FOOL: *(Taking the groat and pleased with his success.)* I thank thee
               much. I'll caper off now, sir.
               (As a final treat.) Pray, keep thy cuckoldry beneath thy
               hat
               And none shall know.
                         (He exits capering and singing, with bells ringing.)
               With a cuckoo, cuckoo, coo!

SELTAZAR: An arrant ass, unworthy of our time.

FORNIA: True, sir, and yet he bred in me a thought:
               'Twas something that the wretch unwitting said.
               (Profoundly.) For oftimes in the midst of idiocy,
               Of foolishness and most inane discourse,
               Mere empty prattle, ramblings imbecile,
               Doth lurk Great Wisdom, perfect as a pearl,
               Philosophy beyond the scope of thought,
               And sageness universal as the sun.
               The fellow mentioned … 'cuckoldry'. My lord,
               Full many years ago when Claudius,

Our King of late, was but an idle prince,
He fell, alas, to lechery and beguiled
A modest matron of the neighbourhood
(Her husband fighting in the foreign wars),
Stole her rich jewel and, when she proved with child,
Abandoned her to the indifference of Fate.
The child was born – a little chubby girl,
The very emblem of a fleshly sin.
The mother, in an ecstasy of shame,
Leapt off a lofty crag and was no more.

SELTAZAR: A lively tale, methinks, to pass the time,
And more amusing than the fool's discourse,
But hardly the solution to our woes:
A land ungoverned and a kingless crown.

FORNIA: That mother was my mother I confess,
And I, my lord, I am the bastardess.
(Pause.)

SELTAZAR: Thou springst of Royal Spawn? Thou art an heir
To Denmark's empty crown?

FORNIA: *(Modestly.)* So I suppose,
Though ne'er before I thought thus to presume.
Still, as you know, by custom and decree,
No woman is allowed to rule alone
In Denmark; she must be be-husbanded:
She Queen and thus he King.

SELTAZAR: So have I heard,
And oftimes thought it full of wise regard.
(Greatly interested.) And … are you thus … be-husbanded?

FORNIA: O sir,
I am no wife nor likely to be so.
No man with favour e'er has looked on me.
(Pause.)

SELTAZAR: To look on you is difficult I trow.
Such blinding beauty: your bright azure eye
Clear as the April morning; your sweet lip:
Dew-struck cherries; the wandering flood
Of your unyielding waterfall of hair;
Your neck, a fair-veined tower of delight
Reaching to heaven; your bosoms lotuses,
More fragrant than their sisters of the sea;
Your lofty brow whiter than Hebe's dove,
Or Nesireena's overcoat of pearl;
Your eyelids, nostrils, elbows, ankles, chins –
Treasures too bright for mortal eye to see.
And yet of them would I the keeper be.

FORNIA: *(Incredulous.)* My lord, you cannot mean …

SELTAZAR: From the first sight
Of you today, my heart has wildly knocked
Against my breast, as eager to escape
And fling itself before your faery feet.
Perhaps you heard it?

FORNIA: No indeed, my lord.

SELTAZAR: Then I shall give my heart a tongue. Dear Fornia,
I love thee. Canst thou look with joy on me,
Freeing me from the hell of damnéd doubt,
And grant me paradise with thy consent?
(Pause.)
And quickly too, before the land is roused
To anarchy or revolution.

FORNIA: *(Enthusiastically.)* Yes, Seltazar, I do consent.

SELTAZAR: My sweetling.
Let us embrace, even as the royal crown
Will soon embrace my new-ennobled brow.
(They embrace, murmuring in pleasure.)

(Musing on his fate.) King Seltazar and thou Queen
     Fornia.

A mighty monarch and his little wife.

A golden reign of justice unalloyed:

The glorious days of Seltazar the First,

Of Seltazar the Great. An era dawns

For Denmark and the world, my Fornia.

The Seltazarian Age is come at last.

     (Pause.)

(Pensively.) And yet, 'twill not be easy to be great,

For heavy burdens weigh upon a king

That humble men know not. For all the night,

Kings lie awake on their golden mattresses

Fretting with care, while every loathsome slave

Sleeps on his dunghill, wrapped in perfect peace.

But, fearless, I submit me to my fate.

(Firmly.) The marriage rites must be performed today.

FORNIA: *(Struck by his masterful manner.)* Very well, my lord, as
     you desire.

A man, new come to court, can do the office.

Friar Laurence of Verona is his name.

He's very good with hasty marriages:

He did the Capulets and Montagues.

SELTAZAR: Did he? Methinks I may have read about it.

Let's seek him out.

FORNIA: Yes, my dear lord. But lo!

See on the ancient battlement nearby,

New gilded by the sunlight of the east

Whose lustres lighten now the clouds' career –

(With dread) The phantom form of Denmark walks his
     rounds!

'Tis Hamlet's father's ghost – in complete steel

Of phosphorescent armour.

SELTAZAR: *(Terrified.)* God defend us!
              *(A faint clanking sound growing ever louder. THE KING
              enters, clad in sparkly armour.)*

FORNIA: A fearsome sight, a dreadful dream of horror.
              And see, he doth approach and doff his helm
              To gaze on us. O, Ghost, we offer thee
              No harm, but only fear. *(To SELTAZAR)* See how he stands,
              Stroking his aged chin with fingers wan,
              Oping his whiskered lips as he would speak.

THE KING: *(Sepulchrally.)* I am the ghost of Hamlet's father, dead
              These past few weeks, doomed to traverse the walls
              Alarming passers-by with hideous sounds
              And ghastly sightings. Or, to be more precise,
              I am young Hamlet's father - but no ghost.
              I speak in a bizarre sepulchral tone
              And wear this curious armour phosphorescent
              And creaking chain mail merely for effect.
              (Dropping his ghostly manner; sadly.) I am not dead, though
                    full of years and woes.

FORNIA: *(Meekly but pedantically.)* I do not wish to contradict a king,
              Especially a late lamented one,
              But rumour hath it and all men declare
              That 'sleeping within your orchard …'

THE KING: *(Interrupting, bored with the story.)* '… I received
              A drop or two of poison in my ear,
              Poured by my treacherous brother Claudius.'
              So the whole ear of Denmark is abused:
              Mine never was. For know that Claudius,
              Reeling with drink as ever was his way,
              In error poured the leprous distilment
              Onto the wrong end of my sleeping form,
              Anointing thus my ankles and my toes
              Which chafe unto this day.

       (FORNIA gasps in surprise.)
       I feigned my death
     And had another buried in my place.
     (Reflectively.) The royal funeral was a stirring scene:
     The pluméd troops, the trumpets and the drums,
     The monstrous cannonade that shook the heavens,
     The tearful eulogies that seized the soul.

FORNIA: *(Surprised.)* But – where you there, my liege?

THE KING: Ay, 'mongst the mourners;
     Though wearing a disguise impenetrable:
     The Lady in Black.

FORNIA: *(Suddenly recalling such a figure.)* You threw a spray of
          flowers
     Into the grave: the weeping violet
     And sad-eyed pansy savouring of the spring.

THE KING: The ceremony o'er, I changed my garb,
     Disguised myself as a perturbéd spirit
     To stride these battlements in my grim attire,
     Groaning and clanking at the midnight hour,
     The better to incite my son's revenge
     'Gainst his incestuous uncle. Which, in time,
     After some hesitation, he effected.
     (Sadly.) A mixed success, for everyone was killed.
     Not only Claudius but Hamlet too
     And Gertrude and the fair Polonius,
     Ophelia and Laertes and the rest.
     A count of corpses most superfluous.
     (He sighs.) So now, my period of mourning past,
     I come to re-ascend my vacant throne
     And straight return to reigning.

SELTAZAR: *(Without enthusiasm.)* Happy news.
     Is it not, Fornia?

FORNIA: *(With great joy, to THE KING.)* Wondrous news, my liege,
Out-topping hope, and healing to the heart!

THE KING: You are the first to whom I've told my tale,
Dear Fornia and honoured Seltazar.
I ask reaffirmation of your pledge,
Your holy vow of steadfast loyalty.
It is my royal wish.

FORNIA: *(Deeply moved.)* Most happily.
My honoured King, I promise …

SELTAZAR: *(Interrupting.)* Good, my liege,
My heaven-rescued, ever gentle sire,
Pray grant me from the bounty of your grace
A moment for some contemplation.

THE KING: *(Magnanimously.)* Of course.

SELTAZAR: I am most grateful, mighty King.
(He moves away, pauses, then speaks in soliloquy.)
And shall I give my loyalty to him,
The feeble emblem of a nation's power?
To lose the crown before I ever feel
Its jewelled girdle round my golden curls,
The sceptre leave unseized, the ball unborne,
The throne unsat upon, the imperial robe
Unstrutted in, the royal rings unworn,
The pomp untasted, and the realm unswayed?
To yield a kingdom – even to a king –
It is impossible! O valour true,
And you, ye engines of ambition,
Arm me with courage and duplicity,
With evil thoughts and devilish stratagems,
Cram me with cruelty fixed and pitiless,
Corrupt my blood and swell my traitorous liver
So that my bile doth burst within my breast,
Tainting each organ with malignity –

My heart a bitter counsellor of hate,
My brain a festering cauldron of foul schemes!
I'll feign obeisance to the King's commands,
Grant him the fealty he fain would own,
But ever plan to pluck him from his place
And claim the throne for Fornia and me.
> *(He goes to THE KING.)*

(Humbly.) I have considered briefly, gracious liege,
And now confirm eternal loyalty.

FORNIA: And I as well, my new returnéd King.

THE KING: *(Moved.)* Thy looks bespeak the honour of thy souls,
Like the soft glove that shows the hand within.
Not like the codpiece which its contents true
Doth mock with gross exaggeration.
(Tenderly.) Great Seltazar and worthiest Fornia,
My heart was never happy till this hour.
Thy loving words hath pierced my agéd breast.
Joy is returned, and once again I feel
The royal blood splash gaily through my veins.
More would I say, but womanish tears intrude,
Filling my eyes and flooding in my mouth,
Drowning all gratitude in sentiment.
> *(He gains control of himself.)*

Pray kiss my royal ring.

SELTAZAR: With pride, great liege.
> *(He kisses the ring.)*

THE KING: I thank thee, Seltazar. And thou, dear Fornia.

FORNIA: *(Greatly affected.)* Of course, your majesty, with loyal lips.
> *(She does.)*

THE KING: And let me press you to my bosom, here.
Good Fornia.
> *(Much moved, he embraces her.)*

Admiréd Seltazar.
(He embraces SELTAZAR.)

FORNIA: We shall be ever faithful whilst we live.

THE KING: I doubt it not. A brief but blesséd time.
(Pause.)

FORNIA: 'Brief' did you say, my gracious liege?

SELTAZAR: Why 'brief'?

THE KING: *(Angrily.)* O, Seltazar, thou vile, ambitious cur!
Insidious slave and rude rebellious hind!
Although it be against all courtesy,
Your whole soliloquy I overheard
And Jove be praised I did. You thought to swear
False fealty and then to steal my life.
But know, sirrah, I preparation took
'Gainst just such treachery.

SELTAZAR: Your majesty …

THE KING: *(Interrupting.)* The jewel in the ring which thou didst kiss
Was smeared with viper's blood and spider's spleen,
With adder's bile and blindworm's fundament.

FORNIA: *(Gasping.)* Gods!

SELTAZAR: *(Gasping.)* No!

THE KING: My breastplate, which you pressed when I
Embraced you, was with poisons stained and soaked,
With cursed hebona, damnéd wolf's-bane, juice
Of witch's melon, bitter devil's gall,
And mallard's pus. And by my reckoning,
You have not seven minutes left of life.

FORNIA: The ring was poisoned?

SELTAZAR: And the bosom too?

THE KING: Ay, sirrah: poisoned they and poisoned thee.
> *(Sympathetically.)* And thou too, Fornia, innocent thou ye be.

SELTAZAR: *(Furious.)* Then know, perfidious shadow of a king,
> That I shall slay thee now!

FORNIA: No, Seltazar!

SELTAZAR: With this, my valiant ever-eager sword
> Which I, perforce, from out its scabbard pluck
> To strike thy head off with one stroke of steel…
>> *(He tries to draw his sword from his scabbard, in vain.)*
> …And make thee ghost indeed.
>> *(He continues to try to draw his sword with great effort.)*
> One moment pray.

THE KING: Thou canst not draw thy sword, O Seltazar.
> Thy limbs are frail, thy force enfeebled quite
> By poison's potent power which thus subdues
> And shrivels every motion, as thy strength
> Dissolves into a baby's. *(Rather grandly.)* And besides,
> There's such divinity doth hedge a king …

SELTAZAR: *(Interrupting, still struggling with his sword.)* But I shall trim that hedge, your majesty.

THE KING: No, you shall not. For by the sacred throne
> Of Ottomile, whose fire-anointed loins
> The gracious heavens…
>> *(SELTAZAR, with a supreme effort, draws his sword at last.)*

SELTAZAR: *(In triumph.)* Ah!

THE KING: …hath blest with glorious …

(SELTAZAR lunges feebly at THE KING. THE KING catches the sword under his arm like a child 'stabbed' in mock-sword play and there it stays. THE KING gasps and staggers.)

THE KING: *(In pain.)* Vile Seltazar, I have an ancient wound,
Long since sustainéd in the Polack Wars,
Embowered here in my armpit's deep recess
(Like the bright fleck within the cowslip's cup),
Near fatal then and never wholly healed -
And thou hast op'd it.
(He falls to his knees, the sword still in place.)
(Profoundly.) But I do prophesy...

(SELTAZAR steps forward and twiddles the sword malevolently. THE KING gasps again and falls on his side, dead.)

(A pause.)

FORNIA: *(Horrified.)* Seltazar, thou hast divested him
At once of crown and kingdom and of life.
No priest to bless, no unction to make pure,
And no grand speech to give before he goes.
O horrible!

SELTAZAR: Alas, I now repent me
Of all my wrath. *(In tribute.)* He was the greatest king
That Denmark – or the world – has ever known.
A soldier, statesman, scholar, mathematician,
Musician, singer, dancer, acrobat,
Astronomer, inventor, theologian –
A lofty mountain on a sullen plain,
A beacon bright and inextinguishable
To all the ages. I die a traitor's death
And follow him with forced, reluctant speed.
(He falls. FORNIA kneels beside him.)

FORNIA: *(Grieving.)* My Seltazar, impetuous love, farewell.

SELTAZAR: Forgive me, Fornia. *(Frankly.)* Let me now confess:
I planned to marry thee, to reign as King,
And then to murder thee, and then to wed

The beauteous Queen of Naples – for a time –
And then her sister Euphonisia,
A lovely maid with pale unblemished cheek
And eye as bright as blazing Hesperus
When first he hangs his lantern in the heavens.
Then afterwards … But slavish life withdraws
As doth the tide in deference to the moon,
Or shadows following the sun's career
Ere Pheobus' chariot wanders in the west,
Or … but no more. We shall perhaps pursue
This conversation in the after-life.
Farewell, my never-love, my nearly-wife.

> (SELTAZAR *dies.*)

FORNIA: Farewell, deceitful, trustless Seltazar.
All men are false, I see. Their watery vows
Lead but to grief and baffle our estate:
A timely lesson learnt, alas, too late.
Yet Death doth strangely suit the tragic scene:
To be is not to be, but to have been.
I die. The poison rises in my spleen
And, climbing up the ladder of the ribs,
Assaults that sacred citadel, the heart,
Which doth surrender sadly. O I die,
And, to the number, add my due of dust.
But look! The eve with solemn streaks of gold
Touches the envious clouds with burnished light.
My history, and Elsinore's, is told,
Of blood and death, of splendour and of spite.
For never was a tale so sadly true
As this of Hamlet, Denmark's Prince, Part II.

> (*Slumping to the floor, she expires, faintly groaning.*
> *The rest is silence, except for some Elizabethan music.*)

> *CURTAIN*

PRINCE LEAR

a prequel

Prince Lear (1994) was broadcast on BBC Radio Three. The cast was as follows:

PRINCE LEAR, John Moffatt
EARL OF KENT, John Shrapnel
GONERIL, Claire Skinner
PRINCESS EUDOXIA, Rosiland Shanks

Directed by Richard Wortley

Characters

PRINCE LEAR

EARL OF KENT

PRINCESS EUDOXIA

GONERIL

PRINCE LEAR

(A sombre flourish of trumpets. Britain, a room of state in the palace. Enter PRINCE LEAR *and the* EARL OF KENT.*)*

PRINCE LEAR: My trusty Kent, the long day growing dim,
Our horses fetlock-worn and weary we
With deeds of hardihood, let us respire
Here in the foyer of the palace hall
And lose an hour in musing.

EARL OF KENT: Yea, Prince Lear.
Soon may we gain some sad intelligence
Of him, thy royal father lately dying,
Great King Grisweldo, Britain's ancient lord,
And of thy due accession to the throne.

PRINCE LEAR: Myself am old, my father older still.
(He pauses, then with a great sigh.) Eftsoons! Dear Kent,
alas! and well-a-day!

EARL OF KENT: Admiréd Prince, great Lear, forgive I pray
This my too-loving care: I fain would know
Why bearest thou a broad and troubled brow
Wrinkled all o'er as is the wimpling sea
Presaging storm.

(LEAR sighs deeply.)

EARL OF KENT: Why come such heavy sighs,
Wafting thy whiskers white like cobwebs blown
In wintry blasts? Happy thy heart should be.
Thou hast a wife matchless since maidenhood,
Princess Eudoxia, beauteous, without flaw,
Three… striking daughters: Goneril and Regan,
And youngest of all and sweetest to thine eye,
Cordelia.

PRINCE LEAR: O alas, my loyal friend,
             Mefears that I have been most cruelly wronged,
             And by a creature in the very seat
             And rostrum of my soul.

EARL OF KENT: Speak more, my Prince,
             Thy words like lightning strike the tinder dry
             Of my old heart enflaming it to fury.

PRINCE LEAR: My worthy Kent, dear inmate of my bosom,
             Great Earl, then know: My royal wife is false.

EARL OF KENT: *(Astonished.)* The fair Eudoxia, soon to be our Queen?

PRINCE LEAR: Alack, 'tis so. Too potent and too sharp
             The proofs against her chastity. She I thought
             Pure as the priestess at Apollo's shrine
             Or morning dew new-fallen is untrue,
             Stained, faithless and insatiable.
                   (He sighs; then with vain longing.) O! that thou
             Dear Kent, so trial-tested, firm of faith,
             That *thou* were woman and my own dear wife.
             Would that thy ample chest be-ribboned now
             With medals, trophies of thy skill at war,
             Were hung instead with bosoms pendulous,
             Proud ornaments of woman's natural dress;
             Thy manly flanks which thou dost oftimes slap
             In hearty boyishness – would they were host
             To sensual curves that undulating wave,
             Inviting dalliance, with all other parts
             That mark a maid or matron. But alas,
             'Tis idle dreaming, airy fantasy,
             And noisome folly.

                   (Pause.)

EARL OF KENT: O most gracious Prince.
             Full thrice ten years I've served thee with a heart

Of open honesty, a soldier's heart
Rugged and plain, though hiding in its depths
A dark and cloistered secret. I, my lord,
Am female.

PRINCE LEAR: *(Stunned.)* Thou? Is't possible, good Kent?

EARL OF KENT: Past doubting, sire. When first a simple maid,
A goggling, giggling girl, I sighted thee.
'Twas life-long love, though far too humble I
For thy great notice. Yet to thee behold
Was bliss, to join thy roistering fellowship
Past wonder, so I posed me as a boy,
A young effeminate page – now through thy grace
Transmuted to an Earl – and long have served
Thy valorous greatness. *(Reminiscing.)* At the first, my Prince,
Manhood was all my study, and long hours
Were passed in learning vulgar oaths and vile
As 'Sblood! and 'Slids! and Zounds! and 'Sdeath! and 'Struth!
And those that would befoul my virgin lips
Now to recount, my maidenhood revealed.
I fought in battles 'neath thy banner bright
And many a Saxon did I disembowel
With slashing lance, and many a traitorous head
Lop off and many a limb. Yet all the while
I longed instead for woman's meeker ways,
To sit demurely in a garden fair
Upon a swing, magnolias in my hair.

PRINCE LEAR: *(Incredulous.)* Thou art a woman, Kent? But I've beheld
Thy manly garb: thy massive helmet plumed,
Thy armoured leggings and thy spikéd belt
Behung with battle-axe and severing sword.

EARL OF KENT: Bought from a man's outfitter, greatest lord.

PRINCE LEAR: Thy hair close-cropped, not silken tresses fair,
        But hacked, like wheaten sheaves at harvesting.

EARL OF KENT: Cut by a man's hairdresser, royal sir.

PRINCE LEAR: But then thy voice: rich, deep, reverberate,
        Sounding the compass mellow to profound,
        Not piping squeaks that pierce the aching ear.

EARL OF KENT: True, good my lord. My voice was ever low,
        An excellent thing in woman, as you know.
        And years of drinking sack and heavy mead
        Have delved for me a deeper voice indeed.

PRINCE LEAR: And yet thy form, thy vast proportions
        Do not proclaim the woman but the man.

EARL OF KENT: The generous use of padding, greatest Prince,
        Of horsehair, leather, sacks of flax and straw,
        And oak and elm and cedar well dispersed.

PRINCE LEAR: A rugged husk to hide a tender fruit
        Delectable. Unlike my royal wife,
        Soft at the skin but marble at the core.
        O cruel, dissembling, false Eudoxia!

EARL OF KENT: Thou spoke of proof against her, dearest Prince.

PRINCE LEAR: Ay, Kent, I shall disclose to thee her shame.
        (Pause.)
        As well thou knowest, good friend, my eldest daughters
        My Goneril and my Regan – e'er have been,
        From earliest infancy, a bitter scourge:
        Splenetic, foul, unloving, sly and sour,
        A pair of scornful furies born to sting
        And agonize the world. Is it not so?

EARL OF KENT: *(Tactfully.)* …Perhaps, my liege. And yet, Cordelia…

PRINCE LEAR: *(Joyfully.)* Cordelia – yes. When she was born she
came –

Not weeping forth as other babies do –
But smiling sweetly, with a grin for all,
A glance of modest, warm, sincere regard,
And tinkling laughter bubbling to the brim,
A sunny disposition – like to mine.

EARL OF KENT: True, greatest Prince.

PRINCE LEAR: She is indeed my child.
            (With gathering fury.) But whose rank loins did father
                  those her sisters,
            What base o'erreaching slave adulterous
            Sowed his vile seed within my furrow fair
            To bring forth sprouts corrupt, degenerate,
            Foul weeds that strangle where they should adorn,
            Unlike to me in promise or in proof
            I know not. *(Pause; thoughtfully.)* And yet thou hast loved
                  me long
            Thou sayest, gentle delicate amorous Kent?

EARL OF KENT: Yes, dear my Prince.

PRINCE LEAR: Then Kent, come to my arms.
            The quest for faithful love concludeth here.
            Fling off thy guise, thy manly false attire,
            That I may thee embrace.

EARL OF KENT: *(Disturbed by LEAR's words.)* My gracious sire …

PRINCE LEAR: But soft! Who doth approach? O 'tis my wife,
            The false Eudoxia.
                  (PRINCESS EUDOXIA enters and approaches them.)

EARL OF KENT: Greetings, royal lady.

EUDOXIA: Greetings, good Kent. And hail, most regal husband.

PRINCE LEAR: *(Coolly.)* My great Princess.

EUDOXIA: *(Most apologetic.)* O sweetest Lear, forgive me!
Forgive me this my absence. *(With joyous innocence.)* I
have been
Strolling in grassy meadows, watching lambs,
Spotless as snow, gambol and frisk with joy,
Emblems of jocund spring; the butterfly
Sips at the dewy cowslip; the young bee
Hums in the rhubarb; gillyflowers bright
Margin the stream, and all the woodland fills
With happy note of throstle and of jay,
Of warbling swallow, and the softer sound
Of bluebells faintly ringing in the breeze.
O'erbrimmed with bliss, I hither skipped to tell
Thee, dearest Lear, of all such miracles
Humble but heartful, and mayhap to woo
Thy greatness out-of-doors, where hand in hand
We'll view Jove's bounteous pageant. Wilt thou, Lear?
What sayest thou, my ever-gentle love,
My darling chuck, my sweetling beyond praise?

PRINCE LEAR: Out, strumpet! Hence, foul hag! Thou sink of sin!
Skein of disease! Infectious harlotry!
Carnal intemperance! Eldest curse of man!
Corruption of the ages!

EUDOXIA: What sayest thou?
Dost doubt my chastity, my noble lord?
What moves thee thus?

PRINCE LEAR: Demon insatiable!
Concupiscence detested, quit my sight!

EUDOXIA: Some error of my making works on thee.
(Humbly.) If I have failed thee, my most sovereign lord,
Noblest of men (for, though a princess I,
A wife's humility is her greatest crown,
Obedience her tiara and her robe,

Unworthiness her sceptre and her throne) –
If I have failed thee, bent not to thy whim
Triumphant, or not willingly debased
Myself to loving vassalage as befits
A woman's frailer nature - watery, weak,
Impure and wavering, lacking man's resolve
And instinct for command – if e'er I have
Presumptuous thus…

PRINCE LEAR: *(Interrupting.)* Silence, despiséd trull!
Arroint! Be off, thou miscreated fiend!
Avaunt!

EUDOXIA: *(With all possible decorum.)* With thy permission,
Gracious Prince,
I thus withdraw. My lord, my Earl of Kent.
(She exits sadly.)

EARL OF KENT: *(Discreetly to LEAR.)* I fear you may misjudge …

PRINCE LEAR: Fear not, my Kent.
The brazen thing has crept away. Once more
Come to my arms, voluptuous Earl.

EARL OF KENT: *(Reluctantly.)* My liege …
(GONERIL enters.)

GONERIL: Sweet sire, my greetings. Thee too, humble Kent.

PRINCE LEAR: Goneril!

EARL OF KENT: My lady.

GONERIL: Dearest Father,
I stand as messenger to bring thee news
Of *thy* great father. *(Pause.)* He is living yet.
Or, to be more precise, is dying yet
And soon will be as dust, as rubble strewn
On the common highway, and you shall be King.

PRINCE LEAR: I thank thee for thy tidings, Goneril.
Where is thy sister, dear Cordelia?

GONERIL: She now is in the country, noble Father,
Smiling at all the peasants, giving alms,
Helping them plough their fields and grind their grain,
Toiling and singing with a merry heart,
Tending to sickly babes, and visiting
The dead and dying with a cheery word.

PRINCE LEAR: 'Twas e'er her recreation, native-led
To goodliness. *(To KENT)* The image of myself
In all save gender. *(To GONERIL.)* And thy sister Regan?

GONERIL: Also in rural byways, mighty Father,
Taunting fair virgins with vile epithets,
Roistering with uncouthest bastardy,
And setting fire to peasants' straw abodes:
Such is her custom in the afternoon.
We oftimes work together.

PRINCE LEAR: Do you, daughter?
(Far away, a great door scrapes open.)

EARL *OF KENT:* But lo! Who comes, her hair entwined in knots,
With ambling gait and handfuls of wild herbs,
And dangling flowers festooning her fair brow,
And wildly rolling eyes, and tattered garb,
With ruff besoiléd, wimple all askew,
Humming old snatches and pulling faces strange
As if in madness?

PRINCE LEAR: 'Tis Eudoxia!
(EUDOXIA enters, humming an old snatch.)
How is it with you, wife?

EARL OF KENT: Good my Princess …

EUDOXIA: Greetings, sweet gentleman, kind maiden too.

> I pray you all a moment's audience.
> For I am the Cheddar Gorge, and in my depths
> Do many creatures dwell who hate the sun
> And fly forth but at midnight to explore
> The sleeping world.

EARL OF KENT: Alas, alas, sweet lady.

EUDOXIA: *(Reciting.)* As the turtle dove in its feathered shell
> Nightly coos on the ocean floor,
> And the wombat wings at the midnight knell
> To its cosy wom once more…
> *(Breaking off into prose.)* Who is the handsome Prince of
> Britain? I would fain speak to him and his vassals twain.

PRINCE LEAR: 'Tis I, good madame. What is, I pray, thy pleasure?

EUDOXIA: Gifts, gifts, good, sir.
> *(Distributing herbs.)*
> There's rosemary, that's for remembrance. There's
> fennel, that's for forgetfulness. There's basil, that's for
> spaghetti Bolognese.

PRINCE LEAR: *(To KENT.)* What wild and whirling words are these?

EARL OF KENT: My lord,
> Such as have meaning to the mind alone
> From which they come.

PRINCE LEAR: Alas, Eudoxia.
> I fear my strong rebuke hath made her mad.

EUDOXIA: Here's flowers for all: the vapid heliotrope,
> The furtive daisy obstinate and rude,
> The dainty-footed columbine, the rose.
> Take thou the thorn without the rose, O Prince,
> And bleed away thy pain. *(To GONERIL.)* Hast ever seen
> The moon within a thimble?

GONERIL: No, my lady.

EUDOXIA: Then eat thine elbow for an apricot,
        For pelicans don't sing.

PRINCE LEAR: Her words are strange,
        Yet uttering a truth that Truth itself
        But barely hints at. Thinkst thou not, good Kent?

EARL OF KENT: Arbitrary as the forest breeze,
        Speaking now prose, now verse, now full quatrains;
        A mixture self-confuséd as the weeds
        That tangle in the murky depths of the sea.

EUDOXIA: Life is a plum, my lord, and death a prune
        Too soft for sucking.

EARL OF KENT: *(Approaching EUDOXIA.)* O my gracious lady…

EUDOXIA: *(Urgently.)* No, come not near, good sir, lest suns collide
and all cosmology lies waste as any oyster. *(Alarmed.)* See, see,
already the woof of the heavens is quite undone and the little
stars go dangling. *(To GONERIL.)* Art thou a mender, madam,
a sempstress of old trappings? Sit thou there and stitch, good
heart, till clouds pass by again and skies unfurl, as in my days
of sweetness.

PRINCE LEAR: Good madam …

EUDOXIA: *(Singing.)* Last night I dreamt of cheese and pippin pie.
        The pie was mute, as though bereft of words.
        The night was dark, yet stars were in the sky,
        And solitary peacocks strode like brightly coloured
            birds.

PRINCE LEAR: Sweet Princess…

EUDOXIA: 'Tis morning. I must get me to the meadow and drink
the dew lest it engulf the world. Yet the open field is
Nature's brothel. The lecherous frogs squat and squirt
and commingle in their common froth abundant, and
the butterfly ravishes the virgin rose.
The nut-hatch doth it with the popinjay,

The crow with the wren, stroking her feathered loin
With his dark bill. Lo! Nature unnatural grows:
The dove assaults the eagle, the meek ewe
Violates the ram unblushing, the new-born colt
Despoils the mighty stallion; all, all, all
Is rife as bawdry, base as wormy earth!

GONERIL: Madam, I pray, becalm thyself a while.

EUDOXIA: *(To GONERIL.)* O you are like the sunflower, dearest lady,
But how, I cannot tell. *(With sudden excitement.)* Hark,
kindly friends!
My airy chariot comes! Its wingéd cows,
Longing to draw it through the unchartered skies,
Moo for employment. O I flee! I flee!
(EUDOXIA flees, running away and laughing pleasantly.)

PRINCE LEAR: Follow her, Goneril, lest she encounter harm,
Or prove conspicuous on the blasted heath.

GONERIL: Verily, great sire.
(GONERIL exits at speed. A pause.)

PRINCE LEAR: *(Sadly.)* O! Eudoxia!

EARL OF KENT: *(Thoughtfully.)* The alteration in her manner sad
Dismays my eyes, great Prince, and stuns my brain:
Is she now sane, pretending to be mad?
Or was she mad, pretending to be sane?

PRINCE LEAR: Now mad and seeming so, though thither drawn
By injured innocence. O Kent, I see
My wife is pure: such madness we beheld –
Melodious, wild and striking, full of strong
And telling images – flows not from souls
False in their faith or senseless of their sin,
But from a heart with wifely virtues stuffed,
As holy as 'tis humble. O I grieve,
For base suspicions prove me truly base,

And comfort have I none beneath the sky.
(He groans.)

EARL OF KENT: *(All compassion.)* Dear Prince.

PRINCE LEAR: O Kent, 'twould soothe my ragged senses
                 And grant me peace, to nestle my sad head
                 On thy receiving breast.

EARL OF KENT: *(Alarmed by the suggestion.)* My worthy Lord …

PRINCE LEAR: Those halcyon waves – thy bosom – are to me
             Luxuriant cradle. There I'll weep myself
             Even to silence.

EARL OF KENT: *(Still alarmed.)* My most gracious liege …

PRINCE LEAR: 'Twould comfort me, my Kent. And presently,
             My sorrow faded and my passion raised
             Above the fathom-line of these my tears,
             I might perhaps … embrace thee, perhaps kiss
             Thy coral lips ambrosial; and then, Kent,
             By conquering lust enflamed and rites of love
             I'd claim at last thy maidenhead.

EARL OF KENT: *(Utterly astonished.)* My lord,
                 Such cannot be, for thou art marriéd,
                 And I an unwed virgin, helpless thrown
                 Upon thy great protection. Honour, Sire,
                 True honour sanctions not adulterous deeds,
                 The shameless meeting of unmarried loins:
                 'Tis treason 'gainst the Kingdom's holy law,
                 Treason 'gainst thyself.

PRINCE LEAR: *(Distinctly disappointed.)* Well said, good Kent.
                 Most loving but most loyal.
                      (GONERIL enters.)

GONERIL: *(In distress.)* Noble Father!
             Great Lear! Kind Prince!

PRINCE LEAR: How now, young Goneril!
                (A pause as GONERIL doesn't speak.)
          What sayest thou, my daughter?
                (Another pause.)
                Thy wide eye
          And mouth agape doth mutely hint at horrors.
          Thy hair up-standing and thy skin as white
          As ivory blanched, and thy stiff arms outstretched
          In stark amazement, and thy trembling form
          Vibrating like the string of some shot bow,
          Or leaf quick-flapping in the wanton wind
          When summer's past, alas suggest the same.
                (Pause.)
          Pause not, but speak to my foreboding ear.

GONERIL: My gracious Father, most reveréd lord,
          I followed my dear mother, saw her range
          The meadows for fair blossoms to augment
          Her late disperséd posy. As she stooped
          To pluck the russet mallow from the bank
          Of the broad brook, she slipped and, flower-like,
          Fluttered into the waters. There she lay,
          A strengthless lily on the placid stream,
          Singing sweet songs and strumming a wet lute.
          The banks were fringed with osier and okra,
          Sweet marjoram, assertive eglantine,
          Soft turtlewort and silvery marrow-bilge,
          Blue saxifrage that sagest matrons use
          To medicine boils and blisters, and that herb
          Called Neptune's folly by the Portuguese,
          Most excellent in salads. Thus she lay
          And, warbling all the while her pensive song,
          She drifted slowly down the dimpling brook,
          Into an inlet, thence a swift canal
          That twisted serpent-like through meadows fair

(Her body bending with the bending stream)
And carried her, still singing lovely lays,
Into the flowing river's widening surge
As faster yet she floated towards the sea,
Borne by the billows in their sparkling play
(The waves engoldened by the setting sun);
Next through the rapids dangerous and wild,
The ever-darkening waters mad with froth,
She speeded on; then, sucked in the whirlpool's thrall,
She spun a while like Fortune's giddy wheel,
Still chanting sweetly, and from thence released,
With sudden power and unremitting force,
Cleaving the water with relentless wing
Like some fleet craft, ill-fortune at the helm,
Approached at last the dreaded waterfall
That roared ahead, and helpless downward plunged
'Midst foam and spray and thunderous waters' rack
Onto the shattering rocks. Her breathless self,
Now silent, sank within the searchless wave.

PRINCE LEAR: So she is dead.

GONERIL: Alas, my Father, yes.
          Her soul is bound for Heaven, and her body
          Is even now consuméd in the sea
          By fishy monsters: shark and behemoth,
          The hydra vile and treacherous sea horse
          Tear at her flesh, and grisly serpents dire
          Gorge their gross bellies on her carcase fair.

PRINCE LEAR: *(Sighs deeply.)*

EARL OF KENT: *(Sighs deeply.)*

GONERIL: *(Continuing her report.)* Her limbs sucked clean by limpets,
                    her bare ribs
          Threaded by sea-worms, and her shattered skull,
          An oyster in each eye-case, deep in sand,

                Slight-shifting with the movement of the tide,
                Lie shipwreck-like upon the ocean floor:
                Sad ending for this royal voyager.

EARL OF KENT: Alas! indeed a piteous spectacle.

GONERIL: 'Twas widely viewed by members of the court.
                Myself of course and Gloucester and young Edgar
                And Edmund too (a lusty gentleman)
                And, from his bed, thy royal father who –
                By sorrow struck to watch with agéd eyes
                The watery pageant of my mother's pain –
                Fell sadly grieving and, the doctors say,
                In that mood died.

PRINCE LEAR: My father!

EARL OF KENT: *(Solemnly.)* Gone, great Prince.

GONERIL: He lies, they say, my lord, a shrivelled mass
                Of majesty, his lengthy beard down-hangs
                As doth thy ivy on the fallen oak
                To ornament decay; your coronation
                Is scheduled for tomorrow.

PRINCE LEAR: Alas again!
                A father perishéd, a Princess drowned.
                (With a sigh.) So, wifeless I must wend me to the throne.
                No nuptial prop to stay my tottering steps.
                (He pauses, then inspired.) Unless… Dear Kent, I am
                        unmarried now,
                A widower, though ancient – soon a King.
                Wilt thou become my bride and rule with me?
                'Queen Kent.' - Sits it not sweet upon the tongue?

EARL OF KENT: *(Overwhelmed.)* I am most honoured, gracious liege. My
                        love,
                Already thine in spendthrift loyalty,
                I give again as dowry. *(Enthusiastically.)* Sweetest Prince,

I'll trade my armour for a farthingale,
My helmet for a queenly diadem,
My bloody dagger for an ivory fan,
My raucous laughter for embarrassed giggles,
My swaggering carriage for a mincing step,
A dainty mincing step, my soldier's heart
Of stone for one as soft and delicate
As moonlit clouds that haunt the sable sky,
My vulgar ribald jests for …

GONERIL: *(Quite appalled.)* No, my lord.
My royal Father, 'tis impossible,
Beyond the shot of precedent and chance
And speculation wild.

PRINCE LEAR: O Goneril,
Fear not, for in disguise the puissant Earl
Has loved me from the time he was a girl.
No man is he, nor ever was I ween,
But wife shall prove, and concubine and queen.

EARL OF KENT: *(In rapture.)* My loveliest Lear!

GONERIL: Alas, it cannot be.
Think on't: he is not equal to thy state.
An Earl become the consort of a King?
The Earl of *Kent*? Cordelia now regards
A royal field of suitors, and 'tis said
That she will wed the mighty King of France
With all his glory, pride and equipage,
Unnumbered castles, adamantine powers.
If she, thy youngest daughter, our Cordelia,
Is courted by a Kingdom, couldst thou be
United to a suburb?

(Pause.)

PRINCE LEAR: *(Quite defeated.)* Strong reproof

Unanswerable. So farewell, dearest Kent;
Never shall Lear thy buxom bosom see,
Nor taste of bliss empyrean. *(Sadly.)* O alas,
No queen, no wife. I needs must bear alone
The massy crown of state. My weary frame,
Already stooped, shall, by this overwhelmed,
Be pressed to th'earth. *(Impulsively.)* Oh gods! It better
      were –
Thrice better were – my coronation past,
To … give away my kingdom.
      (Pause.)

GONERIL: *(Very enthusiastic.)* Ever wise!
O ever sage and sapient! Yea, great Sire,
Once King, the title keep, the burden lose:
Cast odious care and wearying toil away,
Divide thy plenteous kingdom into thirds,
And give it … *(As if thoughtfully.)* But to whom?

PRINCE LEAR: *(Vaguely.)* …. Perhaps my daughters?

GONERIL: Again thou hast, unerring, hit the mark!
The bowstring twangs, thine arrow strikes the centre!
Yet – in the spirit of this new sweet reign,
This smiling time of promise and of peace,
This merry age of generous good King Lear –
Make thy great task the lighter, gentle Father.
(With infectious pleasure.) Tomorrow then, thou crowned
      an hour before,
Disperse thy kingdom 'mongst thy daughters three,
And for delight, a contest I propose.

PRINCE LEAR: *(Pleased by the notion.)* A contest, say you, Goneril?

GONERIL: Aye, great Father.
Give thy best lands, thy choicest territories
To her who loves thee most and tells her love
In terms of highest praise, with metaphors

And grand superlatives, sweet eloquence
Straining to touch thy worth. Too long hast thou
Languished unflattered, though the emblem bright
Of honour far-admired. Let greatest praise
Win greatest prize, so shalt thy eager girls
In loving joy strive lovingly to win.

PRINCE LEAR: *(Delighted.)* Gross flattery as the index of thy love:
I like it much and doubt not it will prove
Brave entertainment. *(With approval.)* And thou, Goneril,
I see that thou at last hath kindlier grown,
Thy icy nature felt a sudden spring
Which greatly pleases. 'Twill be lively sport
And fair beginning. And I prophecy:
Cordelia, loving most and most belov'd,
Will victor prove, and win to her domain
The bulk of the kingdom. What thinkst thou, good
        Kent,
Of this, my Goneril's plan to ease my soul?

EARL OF KENT: *(Strongly disapproving.)* Your majesty, I fear that such a
        course –
Rash and unsifted as the heedless sea
Chafing with foam the indignant rocks …

PRINCE LEAR: *(Reproving.)* Great Kent,
Put off thy frowns, the envious spies of doubt,
And clothe thy face instead in ruddy smiles,
Thy tongue in words of expectation sweet,
For that way gladness lies.

EARL OF KENT: *(Reluctantly submitting.)* True, gracious liege.
I shall inform thy other daughters now
Of that great competition soon to come.

GONERIL: *(Cunningly.)* I prithee, Kent, tell but my sister Regan.
I shall proclaim the rules to dear Cordelia –
My father's favourite, gem of all our land,

Fairest of visage, most divine of form,
Open and generous, trusting … gullible.
(Aside.) I'll cram her credulous ear with counsel, thus:
Our father yearns for plainness in her speech,
For rough-tongued, blunt, unflattering honesty,
Even unto rudeness. O her words will bring
Ruin to her, confusion to the King.
> *(She throws back her head and laughs wickedly and loudly.)*

PRINCE LEAR: I love thy lilting laughter, Goneril.
And am myself inclined to boisterous joy
And heartiest glee. *(Laughs merrily for a moment.)* O 'tis
a harbinger
Of happiness to come. *(With delight.)* Call forth my fool!
We'll list his jests, his riddles and his puns,
And cackle until morning.
> *(A crowd noise, faint at first but growing.)*

EARL OF KENT: But behold!
What massive crowd spontaneous gathers here,
Mixing sweet smiles of pride and loyalty?

PRINCE LEAR: *(Pleased at the turn-out.)* A multitude rejoicing. *(Addressing
the audience as the crowd noise fades.)* O ye
friends,
Who hither come to hail me as your King,
High lords of glory, princely visitors –
Gloucester and Cornwall, Somerset and Essex,
Great Croydon, worthy Basildon, brave Cheam –
Know thou: Despair is passed; beneath my sway,
Justice will mate with Charity, Joy will prove
The happy issue, Joy and lasting Love.
> *(A general cheer.)*
The morrow shall my coronation see,
And Britain split between my daughters three.

Cordelia will her husband choose full soon,
With royal nuptials in the afternoon.
(Jolly ancient music, faintly heard before, grows louder.)
(To KENT.) But hark! The sound of flageolet and tabor,
Of sackbut, crimp-viol, lute and flutenette.
(To the crowd.) My loyal Britons, valiant countrymen,
Sweet subjects, let our revelry begin.
We'll tread a lively measure, one and all,
May shepherds dance and milkmaids join the throng.
The lark returns the crumhorn's echoing call,
United nature sings a single song.
(Tenderly.) Jove bless this realm; let Fortune flourish
            here
And boundless Peace when I am crowned *King* Lear.
(He laughs jovially.) Soon, dearest Goneril, you and I
            shall trip
This stately reel, a gentle partnership,
Like agéd Winter in the arms of Spring.

GONERIL: With pleasure, kindly Father, and great King. *(Unable to control her mirth, she bursts into wicked laughter.)*

PRINCE LEAR: *(Intimately, but well above the sound of the music and the crowd.)*
            But first, sweet Kent, pray join this dear accord
            And dance with me.

EARL OF KENT: *(Doomfully.)* Enchanted, gracious lord.

            (PRINCE LEAR takes KENT's hand and pulls him to him and they dance. LEAR laughs loudly and jovially again, KENT dolefully, GONERIL wickedly. Hearty dancing by all – including GONERIL on her own – as the jocund music grows louder.)

            CURTAIN

FATAL LOINS

Romeo and Juliet reconsidered

Fatal Loins (2001) was broadcast on BBC Radio Four. The cast was as follows:

ROMEO, Samuel West
FRIAR LAURENCE, John Moffatt
JULIET, Rachel Atkins
NURSE, Pam Ferris
ROSALINE, Nancy Carroll
COUNTY PARIS, Ben Crowe
CHORUS, Ray Lonnen

Directed by David Hunter

Characters

FRIAR LAURENCE

ROMEO

JULIET

NURSE

COUNTY PARIS

ROSALINE

CHORUS

FATAL LOINS

(Romantic music which fades away by the middle of the Prologue.)

PROLOGUE
(Spoken by a man or woman.)

CHORUS: Two households both alike in dignity,
A boy and girl by Fortune cursed and blessed,
A look, a dance, a kiss, a balcony,
A wedding, several killings, and the rest;
A tale of fatal loins and famous lines,
Of star-crossed lovers and inept divines.

But O! if stars like theirs could be *un*crossed,
If grief converts to joy and gore to glory,
A message is delivered that was lost
Which alters the direction of our story...
If Juliet and Romeo survive,
Will their eternal passion stay alive?

SCENE 1

(Mantua, a public place. FRIAR LAURENCE approaches ROMEO, both in disguise.)

FRIAR LAURENCE: Prithee, good fellow, you who bustle so
Along these fragrant streets of Mantua,
May I – a stranger here – of thee enquire
For knowledge needful to my soul and me?

ROMEO: In faith you may, O venerable sir
(A merchant rich to judge from your attire),
Though I in Mantua be a stranger too,
Nor of this city nothing know at all,
Yet from the orchard of my ignorance

                  I fain would pluck the sweet, elusive fruit
                  You hunger for.

FRIAR: Well answered, bearded youth.
                  I seek a gentleman Verona-born,
                  The son of a most ancient family,
                  That doted briefly on one Rosaline,
                  But at a ball encountered his true love,
                  A fair and flawless maiden of a name
                  Foe to his own and hateful to his house.
                  He married her, the ceremony brief
                  Conducted by myself. But O! he slew
                  (Alack the day!) her hearty kinsman bold
                  Young Tybalt, and was banishèd from thence;
                  Both banishèd <u>and</u> vanishèd is he,
                  For I have sought him here in Mantua
                  Without nor sign nor savour.

ROMEO: *(Struck by the FRIAR's words.)* Worthy sir,
                  You speak of one twinborn with me to sorrow,
                  Coincidence most prodigal and strange.
                  For I, like him, was in Verona born,
                  Like him once loved a Rosaline, but my heart
                  Fell captive to the daughter of my foe.
                  Again like him I soon did marry her.
                  Like him again I slew her kinsman bold,
                  (He *also* callèd Tybalt), for which deed
                  Was punishèd and banishèd as well,
                  And wander here in Mantua as in Hell,
                  Exiled forever from the Paradise
                  Of Juliet and her heaven-beaming eyes.

FRIAR: *(Delighted.)* O Romeo! Romeo! Therefore art thou
                      Romeo!

ROMEO: *(Surprised.)* 'Tis true, I am. Most pleased to meet you, sir.

FRIAR: But to my sight, thou art not he at all.
            Those bristling whiskers I remember not.

ROMEO: I am disguisèd, lest Verona seek
            More vengeance 'gainst me. This my beard is false.
            Beneath it lies a chin unhung with hair,
            Innocent of razor, rosy as a girl's,
            And blushing crimson lips. Behold!
               (He rips off the false beard.)

FRIAR: *(Gasping.)* 'Tis true!

ROMEO: But who are you who seem to know me well?

FRIAR: I too disguisèd am, lest others mark
            My secret mission here. Lo! I remove
            From off my head the tiny circular wig
            Which hath concealed my tonsure from all eyes.
               (He does so.)
               (ROMEO gasps.)

FRIAR: *(Removing his robe.)* I shed these costly vestments, to
              reveal
            The simple habit of a humble friar:
            A gown of coarsest fibre, and beneath
            A hair-shirt, and a pair of hair-pants too
            For ultimate humiliation.

ROMEO: In faith! 'Tis Friar Laurence, he who joined
            In joy my gentle Juliet to me,
            Though sadly severed since. But why dost thou
            Enquire for me in fragrant Mantua?

FRIAR: I have a message for thee – which at first
            I thought to have entrusted to Friar John,
            But fearing he might meet with some mischance
            Improbable, <u>I</u> bring it to thee now.

ROMEO: A message?

FRIAR: Yea, of utmost urgency:
            Bright blazing news that lightning-like will strike
            Thy tinderous heart to flamehood, words that will
            Instruct thy limbs to motion and thy mind
            To quickening resolve. O Romeo, list!

ROMEO: Tell me at once I pray, good Friar, that I,
            Like to the panther in the eager chase
            Of tender hind, or like the Siberian bear
            Across the tundra raging , or the mole
            Fleeing the aardvark's violent advance
            With hastening stride, may rush upon my goal
            Without delay or pause; no faltering thought
            Shall come between the hearing and the deed,
            But mindless action swift, the arrow shot
            Before the bow be bent. No interim take,
            But tell me now and all.

FRIAR: Well dost thou speak,
            And foul and faint and feckless wouldst thou be,
            Idle of heart, gross slave of lassitude,
            Slow and as slothful as the slumberous slug
            Hast thou not uttered thus. For this my news
            Is of thy Juliet.

ROMEO: Juliet? Speak again!

FRIAR: Know first: thy lady's father and her mother,
            Unmindful of thy nuptials, have decreed
            That she, this day, ere yet the golden sun
            Hath touched the nape of noon – that she must wed.

ROMEO: *(Shocked.)* Must wed?

FRIAR: Alas! must wed…the County Paris.

ROMEO: Wed the County Paris? *(Pause.)* The whole County?
            What? City, suburbs, farmland and the rest?
            How can this be? Will every citizen

Of Paris – burgher, merchant, soldier, all –
Be common husband to my Juliet,
And I alone no portion have of her?
(Bitterly.) 'Tis hard!

FRIAR: The County is a man, my son,
A kinsman of the Prince and much admired,
As in thy settled senses thou wouldst know.
O Romeo, on the flame of thy distraction
Empty the pail of quenching patience.

ROMEO: But what am I to do?

FRIAR: Fear not, my friend.
The wedding to the County shall not be.
For know: 'tis given out that thy sweet bride,
Thy Juliet, is no more.

ROMEO: *(Distracted again.)* What? Juliet dead?
Alas! Then farewell, Romeo! I had feared
Fell destiny with cruel and furtive hand
Would snatch our hopes, so purchased Tuesday last
From an apothecary this vial of poison –
Sweet draught of death and purgative for pain.
But first I'll to Verona and the sight
Of that most dear cadaver who now lies
In Capulets' grim vault.

FRIAR: *(Urgently.)* She is not dead.
Thy Juliet but slumbers, and will stir
In just three hours. I did for her prepare
A sleeping draught from simples simply made:
Musk roses, earwigs, bishop's beard and brow,
Rank gillywort, lack-lustre fumitory,
Capacious cardamom, chopped wing of bat,
And powdered tusk of narwhal. It produceth
All the effects of death save that of dying –
A breathless sleep serene, and she will wake

More fresh and sweet than when she had retired,
A bright Aurora washed with morning dew,
And you and I will greet her in the vault
And hasten her away to liberty,
To endless years of life and love and thee.

ROMEO: O kindly Friar, thy hand I humbly kiss.

FRIAR: 'Tis well I told thee, Romeo, for I ween
Misfortune else had blighted and bedimmed
Thy future and bestrewn thine erring path,
Till a calamitous fate had swallowed all.

ROMEO: May hosts of angels thy endeavours bless.
Here on my grateful knees I do confess
The fear that counselled me is proved a liar
Now I have heard thy message, holy Friar.
(With joy.) O never was a story happier yet
Than this of Romeo and his Juliet.

> *(A burst of the romantic music sweeping us onwards, and fading away during the coming Chorus.)*

SCENE 2

CHORUS: Verona now – where Romeo's fair bride
Stirs fitfully within the family tomb.
Her eyes, once closed in death, now open wide,
The rose, once faded, is again in bloom.
Sweet Juliet wakes, but wakes into a dream
Of joy and passion, gloriously extreme.

> *(Verona, the Capulets' vault.)*

JULIET: *(Yawning.)* I wake, just as the Friar had promisèd.
(Amused.) Ay, me! But what a dream I had! Methought
I woke here in this grisly tomb and saw
My Romeo a corpse, and in his hand

A cup of poison previously sipped.
Then I, in wild despair, his dagger took
And hurled it in my heart. Then came the Friar
And hordes of Montagues and Capulets,
The Friar then telling – at enormous length
And vast detail – the story of our love:
The secret wedding and the banishment,
The message not received, our suicides -
Concluding in a scene of woeful sorrow,
Tears coursing down each agèd parent's cheek,
And Romeo and I espoused in death.
But now I look about and nothing see
Distressful, for my tragic dream is o'er,
And dearest Romeo and the Friar will come
Ere yet the hourglass twenty minutes tells
And carry me to married joys.
>   *(A very loud creaking sound as of a family vault being prized open.)*
>   But hold!
What sound is that? – As if this sepulchre
Were forced to ope.
>   *(Sounds of further movement.)*
>   And what is this I see
Far in the dim verge of the hollow vault?
A figure comes. Alas! 'tis County Paris,
He that I should have wed were I not dead,
Yet dead I am not, although marrièd:
A riddle passing strange, but best explored
In moments of less desperate urgency.
(Firmly.) Close now, mine eyes, and, mouth, withhold
>   thy breath,
Presenting a facsimile of death.
>   *(Gasping, she takes a very deep breath and holds it.)*
>   *(PARIS enters.)*

PARIS: *(Passionate.)* O Juliet! I could no longer stay
Lingering in the churchyard there to weep,
But in thy vault I trespass to behold
Thy yet immortal beauty. Thy pale skin
Soft-silver as the vague and wandering moon,
Thy shoulders shimmering in my torch's flame,
Thy languorous neck, the stem of that fair flower
Thy face, a hyacinth in its height of bloom,
Thy burgeoning breasts I long have longed to press
Like pomegranates for their yielding wine,
Thy slender thighs and undulating legs,
Thyself a gorgeous casket – and within
A jewel ne'er to be known or valuèd.
(With fury.) I curse that rogue and villain, Romeo
Who killed thy cousin, bringing thee such grief
As brought thee, maid, to thy untimely tomb.
(Weeping.) A streaming fountain in a barren court,
A water pot shall County Paris be,
Sprinkling eternal tears upon thy dust
And all in vain, for Juliet will not rise,
Flower that she was, again to mortal eyes.
O for a taste of those soft peerless lips,
Banners of passion, emblems of desire,
Still mocking death in their tempestuous pride.
I'll kiss them ere I go!

JULIET: *(Moans helplessly in apprehension.)*

PARIS: Yet hark! What's this?
'Twas but my fancy, for methought I heard
A grunt of joyous expectation,
So frenzied is the lover's fertile brain.
But now, my mouth, to thy too-tardy task:
Plant plenteous kisses on my Juliet's lips.
        *(He is about to kiss JULIET when a sound elsewhere in the
        vault is heard.)*

Who's there? Behold! A visitor intrudes –
A maid unknown to me. What can she seek
Here in the chill of this dark sepulchre?
I'll hide myself midst shadows numberless
And, unperceivèd, overpeer the scene.
> *(He hides.)*
> *(ROSALINE enters and approaches JULIET.)*

ROSALINE: Ah, Juliet. 'Tis I, fair Rosaline,
That Romeo adored ere thy false charms
And brazen graces lurèd him away.
Thy vault was oped, and so I've hither come
To gaze in joy on thy expirèd self,
To pour abuse in thy insensible ears,
To gloat before thy cold, worm-riddled form –
I warm with life and seething with desire –
To ponder thy wide-worshipped qualities,
To view thy splendours and perfections.
And yet I look in vain. A nose too pert,
A thin and haughty lip, lank hair, weak chin,
Hunched shoulders, bushy eyebrows, face as blanched
As crudded milk, and tiny puffy eyes.
Revulsion floods my soul to think that thou
Had banishèd my Romeo from me.
Vile cockatrice, I would I could thee kill,
But happily, Juliet, I can kick thee still,
And, dead and wilted though thou art, I will!
> *(ROSALINE prepares to kick.)*
> *(PARIS rushes out.)*

PARIS: Hold, hold! Restrain thy foot, audacious maid!

ROSALINE: *(Astonished.)* But who are you? Some robber of the tomb?
Be off! thou vulgar, base-born filthy rogue,
Lower than rat or formless creeping grub,
Viler than scurvy or the raging pox!

Thou spawn of sewers!

PARIS: *(Imperiously.)* I County Paris am.
                    (Pause)

ROSALINE: *(Sceptically.)* Art thou? If thou art County Paris, I
            Am Greater Manchester.

PARIS: *(Indignant.)* Abuse me not
            With scornful jest, thou errant creature bold.
            I be great Paris, kinsman of the Prince,
            And heir presumptive to the Veronian throne.

ROSALINE: *(Appalled.)* Forgive me, sire. I am fair Rosaline…

PARIS: …The former love of hateful Romeo,
            Though disregarded for the greater gain
            Of Juliet.

ROSALINE: *(Grudgingly.)* True, sir.

PARIS: And yet thou art
            Sweet to the sense, as bright to look upon
            As Semele and her daughters of the dawn.
            And spirit hast thou, like the hawk in flight,
            Grace of the swan afloat upon the wave.
            Thine eye stores lightning, and thy voice can peal
            Like sudden thunder; thy thick hair is dark
            As night's own tresses, and thine oval face
            Glows with the wonder of the waxing moon.

ROSALINE: So people often say. And yet, great sir,
            Such praise from one so praised, perfection's self,
            Doth kindle me to blushing, for I be
            A maid unwary of the world's intent,
            A virgin bud unblemished and unblown.

PARIS: *(Admiringly.)* Not Juliet's self so favoured was, or fair.

ROSALINE: Not Romeo, sir, could e'er with <u>thee</u> compare.

PARIS: Enough for now. Come, we'll depart this tomb
        For some more easeful, well-appointed room.

ROSALINE: As thou dost please, my lord.

PARIS: *(Brusquely.)* Ay, come away!
                    (PARIS and ROSALINE exit.)

JULIET: *(Catching her breath with extravagant gasps.)* At last I breathe
                again. O near was I,
        Feigning my death, my death almost to die.
        (With disapproval.) False County Paris and false Rosaline.
        Can hearts so alter, faith so quickly yield
        That were with pledges bought and sighing sealed?
        Such converse heard I between Paris now
        And rudest Rosaline! O heaven, I vow
        That ne'er shall be a wife more fond and true
        Than Juliet…nay, than Mrs Montague.
        (Rapturously.) A villa shall we buy a few leagues hence,
        A little balcony protruding thence,
        A chapel used for frequent christenings,
        An orchard where the lark forever sings,
        A ballroom, several nurseries, and a park,
        Bedchamber, servants' quarters and…
                *(The faint sound of ROMEO and FRIAR LAURENCE
                entering the tomb, though at a great distance.)*
                But hark!

ROMEO: Where art thou, love, in this enveloping dark?

JULIET: 'Tis Romeo at last. *(Loudly.)* My sweet, I'm here!
        (To herself.) Never to part, but ever to be near.
                *(She runs joyously offstage to join ROMEO and FRIAR
                LAURENCE. Romantic music as before.)*

SCENE 3

CHORUS: And so they fled away on love's light wings,
Assisted by the kind, indulgent Friar.
Now twenty years pass swiftly: twenty springs
Of promise, twenty summers warm as fire,
And twenty autumns golden, brisk and fair,
And twenty winters frosty, cold and bare.

In Mantua their villa, rose-entwined,
Grows rich with family. And Juliet
Is older now, though to her gentle mind
Her Romeo remains romantic yet.
But memories of love cannot assuage
The discontent of early middle age.

(Mantua, ROMEO and JULIET's villa. The NURSE sees FRIAR LAURENCE.)

NURSE: Good morrow, reverent sir. Dost business have
With any in this house?

FRIAR: I wish to see
Your mistress Juliet. I Friar Laurence am,
And oftimes visit this dear scene of joy
And family love, to bless its residents
With this, my pious presence, and my prayers.

NURSE: Welcome, good Friar, by my lost maidenhead!
I be the Nurse, newly attending here.
My lady comes apace.

FRIAR: I vow I know thee.
Wert thou not in old Capulet's employ?

NURSE: I was young Juliet's nurse long, long ago.
I swear my soul 'twas twenty year or more.

FRIAR: 'Tis true, good nurse.

NURSE: *(Getting into her stride)* Long, long, long , long ago.
I well recall, i 'God! Such happy days
So long ago. Such good times, in God's bowels!
Such joy, O Jesus sweet! O Christ Eternal!
Such pleasure then, O blessèd Trinity!
In St Paul's kidneys! Such times, Holy Virgin!
      (Pause)

FRIAR: Where is the Lady Juliet?

NURSE: With the children.
A-nursing them, as once I nursèd her.
O how she loved to suck upon my dug
For hours and hours, and play and fondle it
And mould it to a thousand curious shapes.
'Give me thy dug!' quoth she both night and day,
'Thy dug, O Nurse!' And seize and pull and twist
As 'twere a doll, and then be-squeeze my teat
And cry, 'Thy dug! Thy dug!' and splatter milk
All round her mouth and chin and forehead too.
And then about the room – the very walls
And ceiling dripped withal. 'Thy dug!' quoth she,
'Thy dug! Thy dug!'

FRIAR: Enough I pray, good nurse,
No more. Thou knowest I am a man of God,
Nor rudely relish anecdotes like these.
Such talk despoils the heaven-delighting soul
And flingeth Hell upon it. Prithee cease.

NURSE: There was a time, good Friar, when thou wouldst look
With passing admiration on my dugs.
Then were my bosoms in their ample pride,
A pair of lilies whiter than the swan,
Each brightly nippled. Downwards wouldst thou glance
When offering the wafer to my tongue,
Thy appetite increasing.

FRIAR: 'Tis not so.
I am a humble servant of the faith,
Stranger to lust and the longings of this world.
My pleasures are in pain and self-denial,
In meekness and in toil and abstinence,
And bitter, uncomplaining sacrifice…
But lo! Thy mistress, fairest Juliet comes.

(JULIET, now grown quite immense, enters. As she does, the door offstage opens briefly and we hear the sound of very many shouting children as in a great echoing room – then the door closes and the noise ceases.)

JULIET: Welcome, good Friar.

FRIAR: Heaven bless thee, Juliet.

JULIET: Go, Nurse, prepare the children ere they meet
The saintly Friar. Make them neat and spruce
And smart beyond reproof.

NURSE: Ay, mistress mine.
(To the FRIAR.) I needs must groom their thickly knotted hair;
They scream at first, then smile to look so fair.
For combing is a kind of pleasant woe,
And parting such sweet sorrow. I must go.

(THE NURSE exits, opening the door – again the sound of numberless children – then closes it.)

FRIAR: So many little ones of every age –
Alfredo, Giovanni and Bianca…

JULIET: *(Taking up the list.)*…Musetta, Guido, Bescalo and Tremi,
Sylvestra, Octorino and Renata,
Claudio, Ferabosco and the triplets.

FRIAR: Most blest art thou and Romeo.

JULIET: *(Continuing.)*…Sophia,

Falopia, Angelica, Rigatoni,
Nardinia, Marcellina and Modesta,
Marco, Picca, Servio and the babies.

FRIAR: So sweet the tender fruitage of the womb.

JULIET: They grow so very quickly, holy father.
               (Pause.)
Alas! yet not so quickly as myself.
Behold! I have grown spherical and orbed,
Round as the moon and heaving like the deep
When Cynthia gathers up its trembling tides
To overflow their channels. Great am I:
No stool, no chair, no sofa can suffice
To bear my mighty bulkage. As a girl
I was as gossamer, hither and thither blown
By light contending winds. Now 'tis not so,
And Romeo – he hath noticed it I know.

FRIAR: Becalm thyself, my child.

JULIET: *(Desperately.)* O Friar Laurence,
I barely fit within my balcony:
It pinches here, and here.

FRIAR: Dear Juliet…

JULIET: But ever pressing on me with a weight
Thrice heavier than myself is one great fear:
That Romeo, repulsèd by my form,
Finds solace with…another.

FRIAR: *(Shocked.)* …Who, my child?

JULIET: I know not I. Perhaps some former love.

FRIAR: But he from former loves is banishèd,
For all Verona lies beyond his means.

JULIET: Then he may be enamoured of a dame
Less distant. Yea, perhaps it is the Nurse.

> Her dugs, she says, are irresistible
> To men of every age and every clime.

FRIAR: If <u>thou</u> attract him not, I little deem
> The Nurse with all her dugs could lure him hence.
> Nay, nay, my child, thy Romeo is true.
> I vow my life on his abiding faith.

JULIET: *(Not to be put off.)* Some pampered jay, some flaunter of
>   the flesh,
> Some Jezebel with painted eye and cheek,
> With slender hip and long curvaceous thigh
> Hath webbed him in her subtle net of wiles,
> And they go at it daily. He at home,
> The perfect spouse and father. Out he slips
> And slips it in, and she insatiate
> Cries evermore for more, her body glows
> And shifts and heaves in bestial ecstasy –
> 'Neath velvet sheets or in the open air,
> In furtive alley or in chamber dark,
> Unceasingly he sows his sinful seed
> In foreign fields, and gathereth she the grain
> That should be for my milling.

FRIAR: No, no, no!
> It is not so, it cannot be, my child.
> Yet, for thy sake, I'll nose the matter out.

JULIET: Wilt thou, good Friar?

FRIAR: Ay, dear Juliet.
> This afternoon meet I with Romeo
> There in thy little chapel on the grounds
> To list to his confession. I shall press
> Most fervently upon the very core
> And crux of this, his dubious offence –
> Though certain am I, daughter, 'tis the weft
> And fabric of thy troubled fantasy.

JULIET: I thank thee, Friar.

FRIAR: Yea, Juliet, all is well,
As Time and thy true Romeo will tell.
Now to thy children, that I may them greet
With psalm and saying, combination sweet.
(The door is opened, again the echoing sound of children.)

SCENE 4

(Mantua, the Chapel.)

FRIAR: A fine confession, Romeo, crisply spoke,
And full of deep remorse.

ROMEO: I thank thee, Friar.

FRIAR: But hast thou listed all thy present sins?
Didst thou not leave some portion of thy soul
Untented and unbreached?

ROMEO: Methinks not, Friar.
All acts immoral I have chronicled
As ever to thine ear.

FRIAR: And Juliet?
Art thou yet loyal to thy loving wife?

ROMEO: I am as ever steadfast unto her.
For witness thereof, I refer, good Friar,
To all the babes our loins have gendered forth
O'er twenty years of spawnage: Giovanni,
Renata, Octorino, Ferabosco,
Sylvestra…

FRIAR: Nay, no list I pray, for I
Have christened all, a dear and constant duty.
But tell me more, if more there be to tell,
Of shame or dark intent, of love denied
Or lust permitted, passions infamous,

Illicit tidings, secrets of thy soul.
(Sensing that ROMEO is wavering.) Thy words, my son, will
        never be disclosed.
'Tis but between thyself and me and God,
And angels in the firmament, and ranks
Of cherubim unseen, and seraphim
Innumerable, and troops of holy saints,
And patriarchs and martyrs of the Church,
And Christ and his immediate family,
And shall no further go.

ROMEO: Not Juliet?

FRIAR: Nay, son, not Juliet, I swear it so.
              (Pause.)

ROMEO: *(With difficulty.)* I love her not. No longer doth my heart
Sing sonnets at the altar of her eyes.
She is much changed. Hast thou perceived it not?

FRIAR: She is a lady pious as a nun.

ROMEO: And vast as a cathedral, holy Friar.

FRIAR: 'Twas bearing thy prodigious progeny
(Sweet gurgling girls and boys of every age)
That hath enlarged her to her present bounds.

ROMEO: Should she not thereby grow the smaller? No.
The more she doth produce, the more she is,
For both are infinite.

FRIAR: Confess, my son,
Is there another that thou favourest?

ROMEO: Truly I have been tempted, gentle Friar,
Even to the port and harbour of the act.

FRIAR: By one alone, or by a vast array?

ROMEO: By one…that I have known these many years.

FRIAR: 'These many years'! Alas! it is the Nurse,
            Whose coarse and bawdy language hath unbound
            Thy fettered sense and rigorous resolve
            And lured thee into sin.

ROMEO: 'Tis not the Nurse.

FRIAR: 'Tis not? *(The truth dawning.)* But one that in Verona
                      dwells?

ROMEO: *(Guiltily.)* Ay.

FRIAR: One thou knew ere thou met Juliet?

ROMEO: Yes, Friar Laurence.

FRIAR: Then it <u>Rosaline</u> is –
            She that thou spurned to marry thy sweet bride.
            I see it in thine eyes. It blazeth forth.

ROMEO: *(Much moved.)* O Friar Laurence, cease! I cannot speak.
            My heart is in my mouth.

FRIAR: Then set thy mouth
            Within thy heart that it at last may tell
            The story of its passion.
                      (Pause.)

ROMEO: *(Suddenly.)* O 'tis thou!
            'Tis thou, dear Friar, 'twas ever ever thou!
            Thy noble qualities have long seduced
            My heart and senses to a love of thee.
            Such purity of purpose, courage, zeal,
            Sweet service – marrying Juliet to me,
            Finding me in fragrant Mantua,
            Thy message given, the fondness it expressed,
            Thy constant aid and counsel e'er bestowed,
            Thy many lofty virtues all bespeak
            A man of spotless saintliness sublime.

FRIAR: *(Shocked.)* Knowest what thou hast uttered, Romeo?

ROMEO: But, Friar Laurence, 'tis thy <u>person</u> too:
Thy rugged visage, wise and strangely plain,
Thy piercing eyes, complexion without stain.
Thy tonsure - that sweet circle past compare,
Like a pink lotus in a sea of hair.
Thy noble ankles and the very toes
That peep out of thy sandals in neat rows.
Thy burly torso that unites and joins
Thy lovely limbs unto thy lanky loins,
Thy loins muscled with kneeling when at prayer,
Thy sultry voice seductive and so rare
When singing hymns or speaking of the Faith,
Of Sin or Life, or anything thou saith.

FRIAR: *(Horrified.)* Fie! Fie! For shame, good Romeo, speak no
more!

ROMEO: O such a love is sanctified by Time.
Yea, here in Italy in ancient days
'Tis said, Great Caesar, Emperor of Rome,
Loved a young man, a slave from Syracuse
Or Ephesus, and oft the two would meet
In court or palace, sunken bath or glade
For sport and dalliance and the rites of love,
And Dromio and Julius were their names.

(FRIAR LAURENCE groans in disapproval.)

For Love's a dainty fairy nimbly fleet
Who tiptoe strides the eye-beams that unite
The gaze of sweethearts. Cupid is his name
And links the loins of lovers everywhere.
Then link we for a bliss beyond compare.

FRIAR: *(Utterly revolted, in soliloquy.)* So terrible his words, more
black and dire
Than septic toads and adders. Flames of Hell
Accost mine ears; fain would I, screaming, pray,

And rend my breast to tatters. But no, no!
I needs must feign a…vague flirtatiousness,
Lest I alarm him and discard thereby
The treasure of his trust. *(Pause.)* I shall transform
His lust for me to love of Juliet.
>   *(He thinks for a moment; then triumphantly.)*
A subtle scheme is building in my brain,
Which cannot fail.
>   *(Aloud.)* My gentle Romeo,
Meet me this evening in my cell, and I,
To your request, will give a full reply.

ROMEO: *(Full of hope.)* The destiny and scope of my desire
Lie firmly in thy lap, vivacious Friar.
I feel as giddy-headed as a boy,
And now shall skip about for very joy!
Farewell, Friar Laurence.

FRIAR: Farewell, Romeo.
>   *(ROMEO exits skipping.)*
The demon in his breast I shall expel,
Like Lucifer from Heaven. But first methinks
'Tis best that Juliet knows all will be well,
And well attires herself for love's return
In beauteous garments rich and flattering.
>   *(Enter the NURSE.)*
Ho! Ancient Nurse. Where be thy lady now?

NURSE: She's presently at feasting, goodly Friar.
Attend her here, she'll not be long.

FRIAR: I shall.

NURSE: Well I recall – O what a memory
Is mine i'faith! – how once I waited long
For my dear husband. 'Twas in mid-July
Beneath a mulberry tree in heavy rain
In north-east Lombardy, from four o' the clock

To midnight, near to Lammas Eve it was,
Or Angus-tide or St Leticia's Day
Or St Ubalda's Pentecost…

FRIAR: *(Bored.)* I must go.
I'll leave thee with a message thou shalt give
To Juliet – which even now I write.
(He begins to scribble a note.)

NURSE: A message, say you? Well do I remember
The message I gave Romeo from thee:
That thou wouldst marry him and Juliet,
A hasty ceremony in thy cell.
The wedding night was full of lusty sport
And jocund gambols on the bed of love.
(I oped the door and briefly peepèd in.)
Such feats mere flesh can do!…

FRIAR: Here be the message.
(He hands the note to the NURSE.)
And now, good day.

NURSE: Good day, thou honest Friar.
(FRIAR LAURENCE exits.)
This note will I deposit 'twixt my dugs
For greater safety, ere I it deliver
Unto my mistress.
(ROMEO skips back into the scene.)

ROMEO: Nurse, what hast thou there?

NURSE: A message from Friar Laurence, goodly master.

ROMEO: 'Tis even so, for well know I the hand
      (And fain would know it better). Give it me.
              (THE NURSE hesitates.)
      (Insistently.) And now, I pray.

NURSE: *(Giving the note to him.)* So be it, gentle sir.
      (With enthusiasm) O i' God's bowels! how well do I
          remember…

ROMEO: I would thou wouldst forget all thou rememberest,
      Remembering only that thou shouldst forget.
      Be off, and do some greasy menial chore!

NURSE: *(Stung by his words.)* E'en so, my lord. I'll ne'er
       remember more.
          (THE NURSE exits.)

ROMEO: And now to read his words and plumb his heart.
          (He opens the paper.)
      'My dear' – so happily doth the note begin –
      'Thy love will be to thee as thou desires:
      Impassioned, ardent, wilful, trusting, bold.
      I bid thee clad thyself in trappings bright,
      In soft and sumptuous garments that allure:
      A farthingale that flutters o'er the floor
      Tight-tapered at the waist, the bodice low
      To startle and entice, thy hair in locks
      Of massy gold besprinkled with pink pearl,
      Necklace of jet, an agate at each ear.
      Thy secret places scent with perfumes rare:
      Pressed cassia from fabled Zanzibar,
      Seared lotus-bud from dusty Marrakech,
      Crushed marigold from odorous Hartlepool.
      Thy cheek resplendent with the rose's hue,
      Thy eye long-lashed with lid of azure tinct,
      Thy lip dyed darker than the cherry dares:
      The very soul of Nature's Feminine,

Sight irresistible to manly eye.
Faithfully yours, Friar Laurence.' O my sweet!
Adornèd so, I soon with thee shall meet.
    (Romantic music, as the scene ends.)

SCENE 5

CHORUS: And so doth Romeo rummage (all on fire)
        Bright finery to find. As Juliet waits
        For wonders to be born, for old desire
        To blaze again, and prays to all the Fates,
        Her husband leaveth home as though 'twere Hell,
        His Heaven to seek in Friar Laurence' cell.

(Verona, FRIAR LAURENCE's cell.)

FRIAR: Soon Romeo enters this, my humble cell,
        And so my stratagem at last unfolds.
        I have prepared for me a sleeping draught
        To swallow on the instant. Romeo,
        Beholding me unbreathing on my couch,
        Will deem me dead. O doubtless he will grieve,
        With many a sigh returning sadly home,
        Where Juliet in dress provocative,
        Fragrant and tempting, heavy with allure,
        Will comfort give and, with th'oblivion sweet
        Of spousal pleasures, win him back again.

ROMEO: *(Offstage.)* Sweet, comely Friar, 'tis I!

FRIAR: And thus I take
        The slumberous potion, but will soon awake.
            (He swallows it, and retires to his couch. Enter ROMEO,
            dressed, accessorised, bewigged and made-up in accordance
            with the FRIAR's note.)

ROMEO: Belovèd, I am come! *(To himself.)* What do I see
        There by the balcony window? Ah, he lies

Reclined already on the amorous couch
Awaiting fond endearments, his coarse robe
Ruffled just so along its ragged hem
To show the ankles in their lusty pride.
(Aloud.) Behold! I am adorned as thou required,
My cheek of crimson tint, my lips a rose,
Swathèd in silk and peppered o'er with pearl
And primed and aching for the act of love.
                (Pause.)
Yet thou art silent, sweet, replying not.
Such coyness doth enflame my rough desire,
Arousing me the more, coquettish Friar.
I'll charm thee with a whisper in thine ear
Of roguish wit and dear indelicacy.
                (He starts to whisper something to the FRIAR, then stops.)
(Shocked) Alas, but what is this? *(In despair.)* O, fairest
                love!
Thy silence speaks of cold mortality,
Thy coyness is the reticence of death.
Ne'er shalt thou know the wild, love-wafting eye,
The heaving hip, the pleasure-thronging thigh.
O rarest rose now lost amidst the briars,
My flower of flowers and my Friar of friars.
So once again, poor Romeo, thou must die.
No dagger bear I to dispatch myself
Here at my silken side. But there's a means.
For in this locket round about my neck
Doth hang a dram of poison in a vial.
'Twas purchasèd from an apothecary
In Mantua full twenty years ago
And carried as a keepsake ever since.
I hope 'tis not gone off. I drink it now.
                (He swallows it with a gulp.)
Ay me! It flows with fiery speed through all
The channels, ports and flanges of my veins.

Now I remember me: the seller said
The poison hath but one adverse effect:
It maketh one to sneeze. *(He sneezes.)* And so it doth.
A violent and quick discharge of breath. *(Sneezes again.)*
O emblem apt and fitting of great Death. *(Sneezes.)*
Such pertinence my soul doth truly please:
Slaying myself, to die upon a sneeze.
       (He sneezes again – a great echoing sneeze – and dies.)
       (JULIET enters.)

JULIET: What sound is this, far echoing through the air
Like hoot of owl or spirit's quavering cry?
I – Juliet – have speedily pursued
A woman dressed in sumptuous garments bright,
Fleeing the chamber of my Romeo
Unseen, or so she wist, and find myself
Here in Verona in the Friar's cell.
What is't I see? The goodly Friar there lies.
His form is lifeless, and his kindly eyes
Are closed as if to meditate on Death.
His holy heart, I fear, hath wholly stopped;
The sermon of his blameless life is o'er.
       (Pause; then with surprise.)
But soft! Nearby, the strumpet that I followed
From Mantua down many a tangled street
Lies slumbering on the floor in deepest rest.
(With disdain.) O tainted wretch, thou false and wanton
       shrew,
Luxurious trull, I know well what thou art.
(In sudden amazement.) No! No! 'Tis Romeo, clad in
       whispering silks,
With stainèd lip and grossly reddened cheek,
With azured eyelid and with flaxen wig!
My love, awake! *(She touches him.)* Alas, his hand is cold.
And at his powdered bosom where the scent
Of marigold yet lingers, his great heart

No longer beats! Alack, what can this mean?
O Juliet, all meaning means but this:
I must pursue him to eternal bliss.
The fatal instrument is not remote.
For, running from the kitchen where I sat
A-slicing onions for our evening meal –
Lasagne verde in a caper sauce
With forest mushrooms – heedless I came hence
With yet the knife in my forgetful hand.
(Bravely.) Into my flesh, thou sharp unsparing knife:
End Juliet's misery now with Juliet's life.

       (She stabs herself, to no great effect.)

Not dead? Alas, too thick the layers be
Of fatty tissue that environ me.
I'll stab me here!

  (She does, without success.)

  And here!

    (She does.)

      And here!

       (She does.)

        And yet,

No death at all for joyless Juliet.

     (She glances about.)

(Inspired.) The balcony - from which the Friar wouldst
        preach
To passers-by, and holy precepts teach.
A balcony! 'tis where our great romance
Began. Now there it ends, by bitter chance.
I'll fling myself from off its lofty height
To plunge at last to everlasting night.
(To Romeo.) Farewell, farewell. Our blazing sun is set.
No longer Romeo <u>or</u> Juliet!

    (On "Ju-li-et!" – and with a cry – she runs to the balcony
    offstage and leaps from it. There is a truly tremendous

> *thud, the impact of which rocks* ROMEO's *dead body and rouses* FRIAR LAURENCE.)

FRIAR: *(In horror.)* What was't? An earthquake cracking Nature's
　　　　　floor?
Or roaring thunder when the lightning strikes
And splinters forests? Or do oceans rise
In crested waves and, breaking, bear away
Whole mountains? Or do spinning suns collide,
Wrenching the planets from their ancient course
To bring back Chaos?
> *(He looks through the window.)*
　　　　　No, 'tis Juliet
Fallen from the balcony.
> *(He studies her briefly, and reports back.)*
　　　　　She lifeless lies,
No breath at all in that gigantic frame.
With bloody stabs in breast and thigh and flank,
Each wound a mouth wide-gaping at the deed,
Or like a choir full throated singing loud
A requiem for her still-soaring soul.
Bless thee, dear lass.
> *(He notices* ROMEO.)
　　　　　But who is this I see? –
Similarly dead, a far more lovely maid,
In garments that allure the manly eye.
A cheek that shames the rose and leaves it pale,
Petals for eyelids and an ivory brow,
Dumb lips that speak of prospects more divine
Than any offered in mortality,
Stirring the soul to a rapture beyond joy.
Down, down, O down, my too-long-slumbering heart!
Never knew I true love until tonight.
My mind, my life, my very soul is fixed
On her forever, though alas! she's gone.

(Looking more closely.) Alas! alas! alas! She's Romeo,
Now transubstantiated to a girl!
'Tis he inflates this passion in my breast
And brings me to the summit of desire,
And he a man and I a holy friar!
O heaven! My soul is maddened, lost, amazed,
Infected, blackened irredeemably
For love of wild, bewitching Romeo.
I blame him not. 'Tis I alone, 'tis I
Who lit the flame of longing in his loins,
A flame fatal to him and now to me,
To me and to my own tormented soul.
            (Romantic music comes faintly in.)
(Enraptured.) And yet, so strong this miracle of romance,
This swell of passion singing in my breast,
The dear delight that in my soul doth dance –
No love so sweet in th'east, south, north or west,
In Rome or Venice, Genoa or Florence,
As of <u>my</u> Romeo and <u>his</u> Friar Laurence.

> *(FRIAR LAURENCE sighs with passion, as the romantic music grows louder.)*
>
> *CURTAIN*